DEDICATION

Much Love To My Mom

Beatrice

And To Those of You

Coloring Outside Of the

Lines

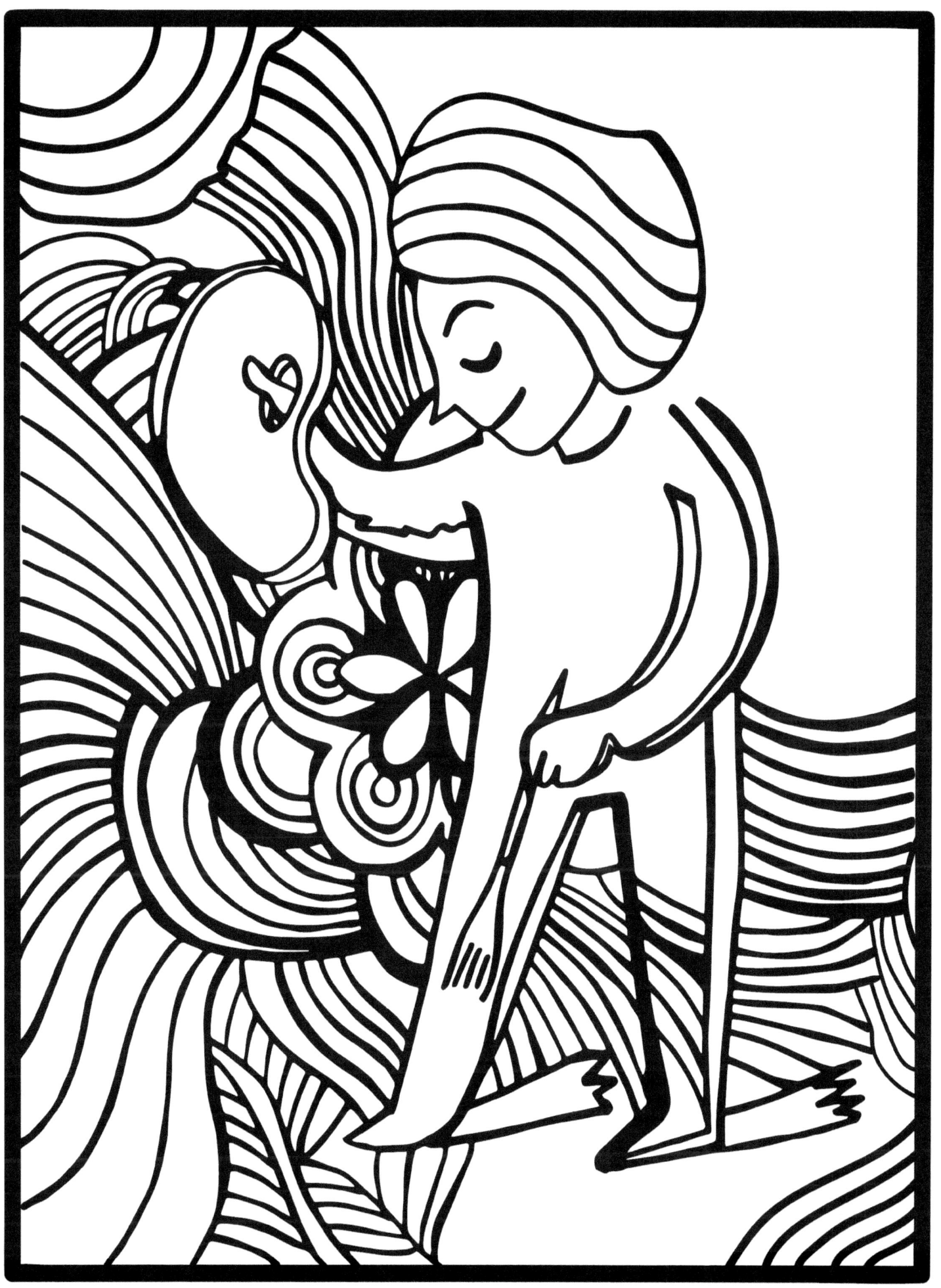

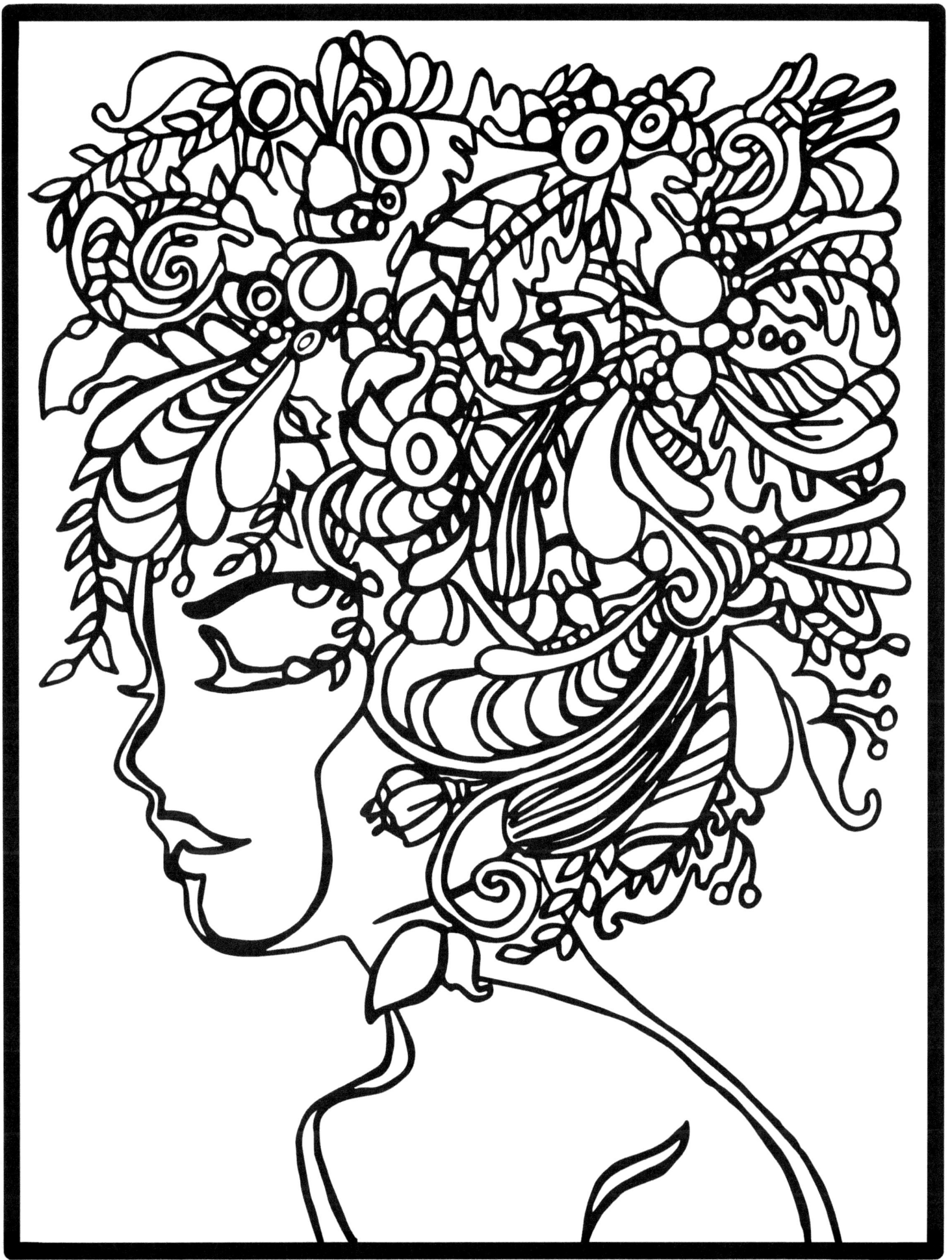

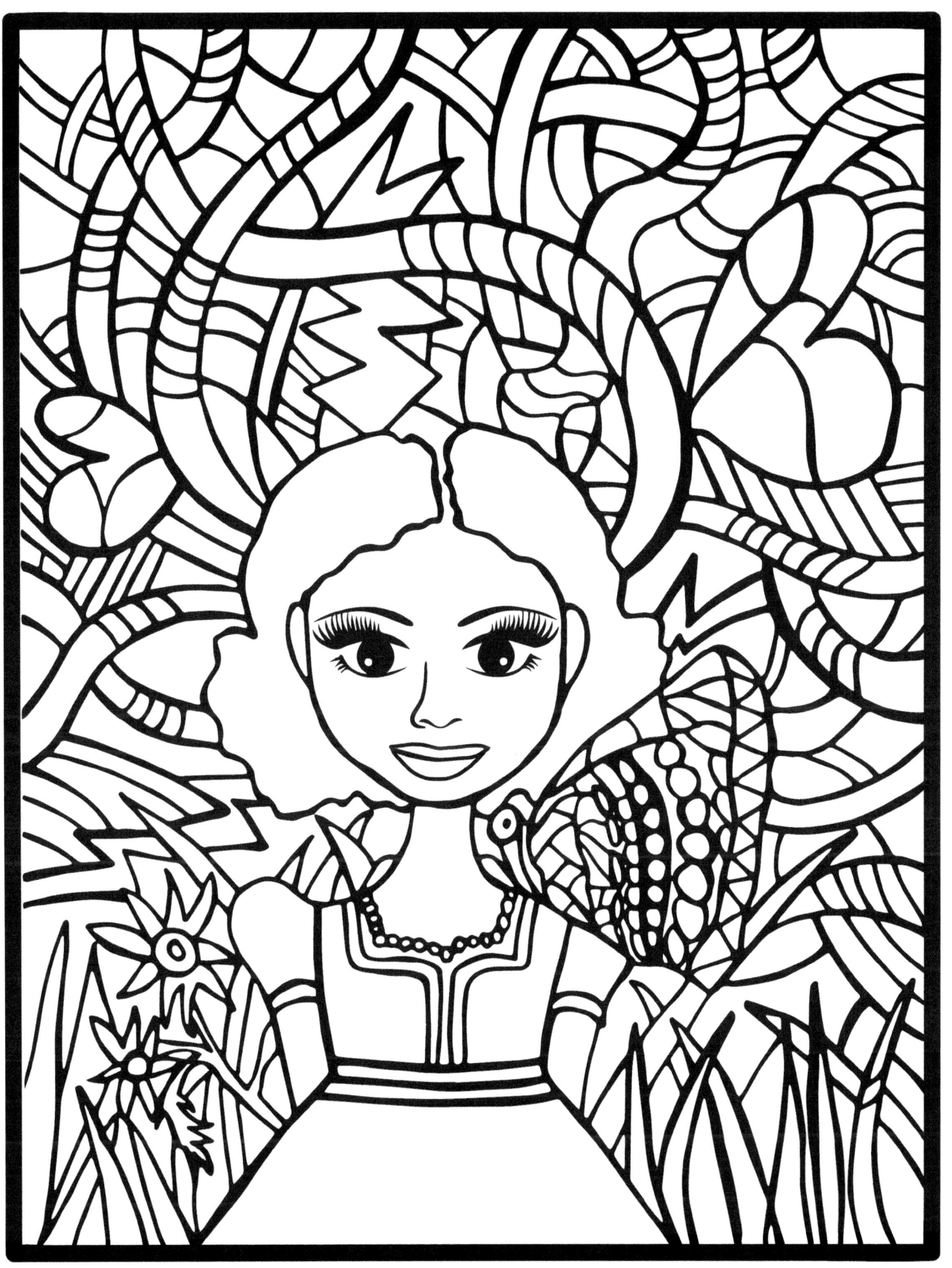

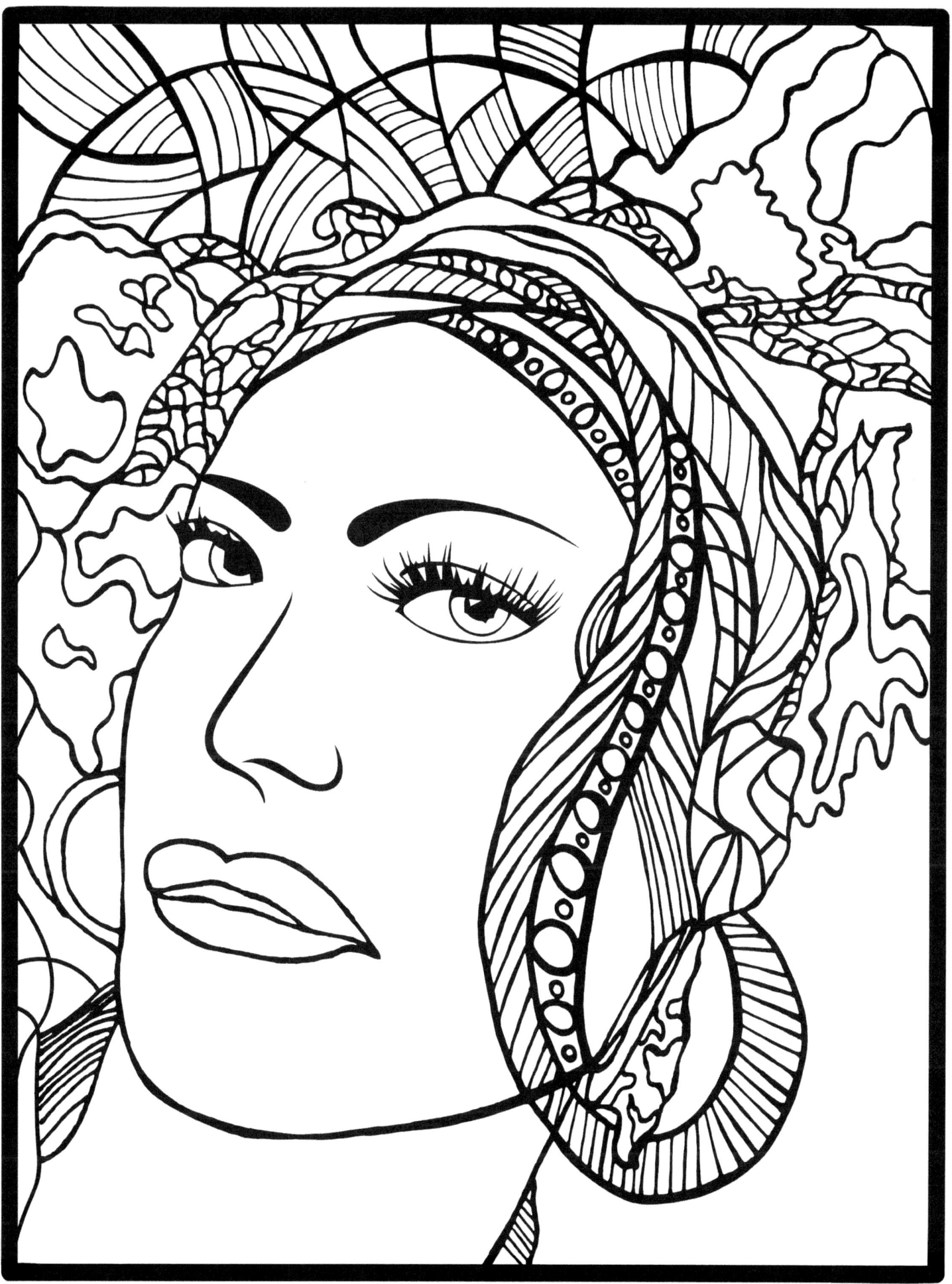

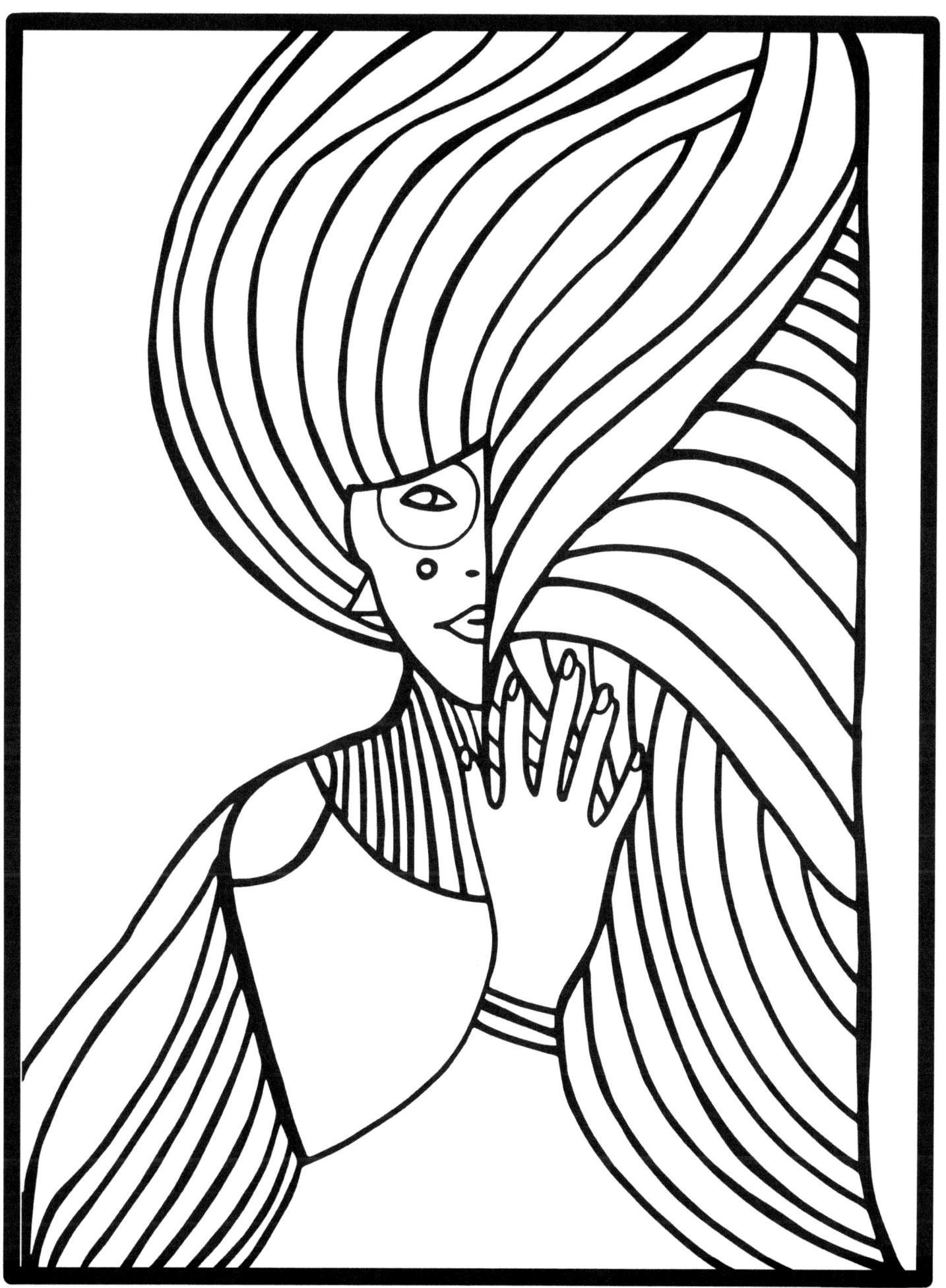

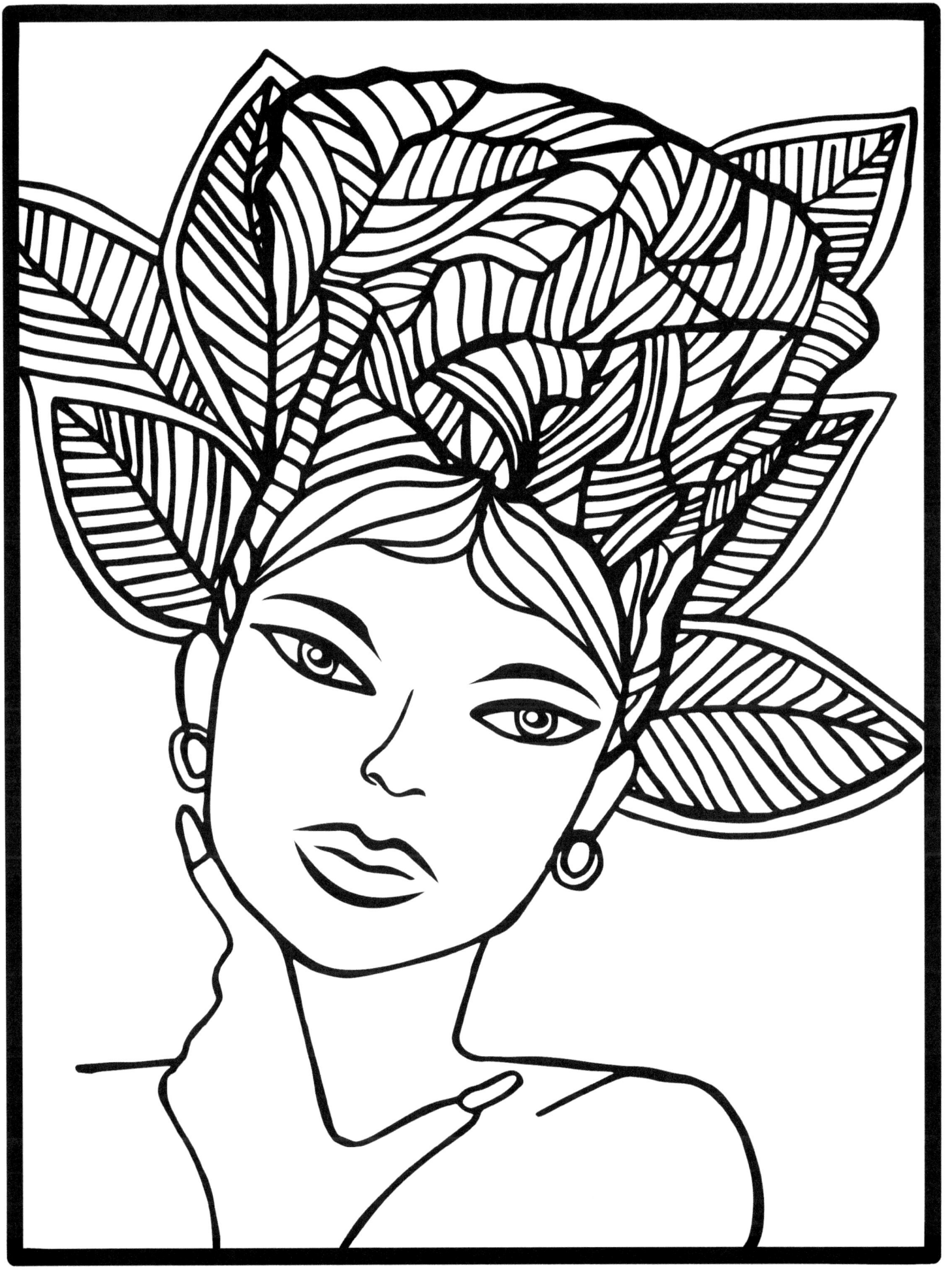

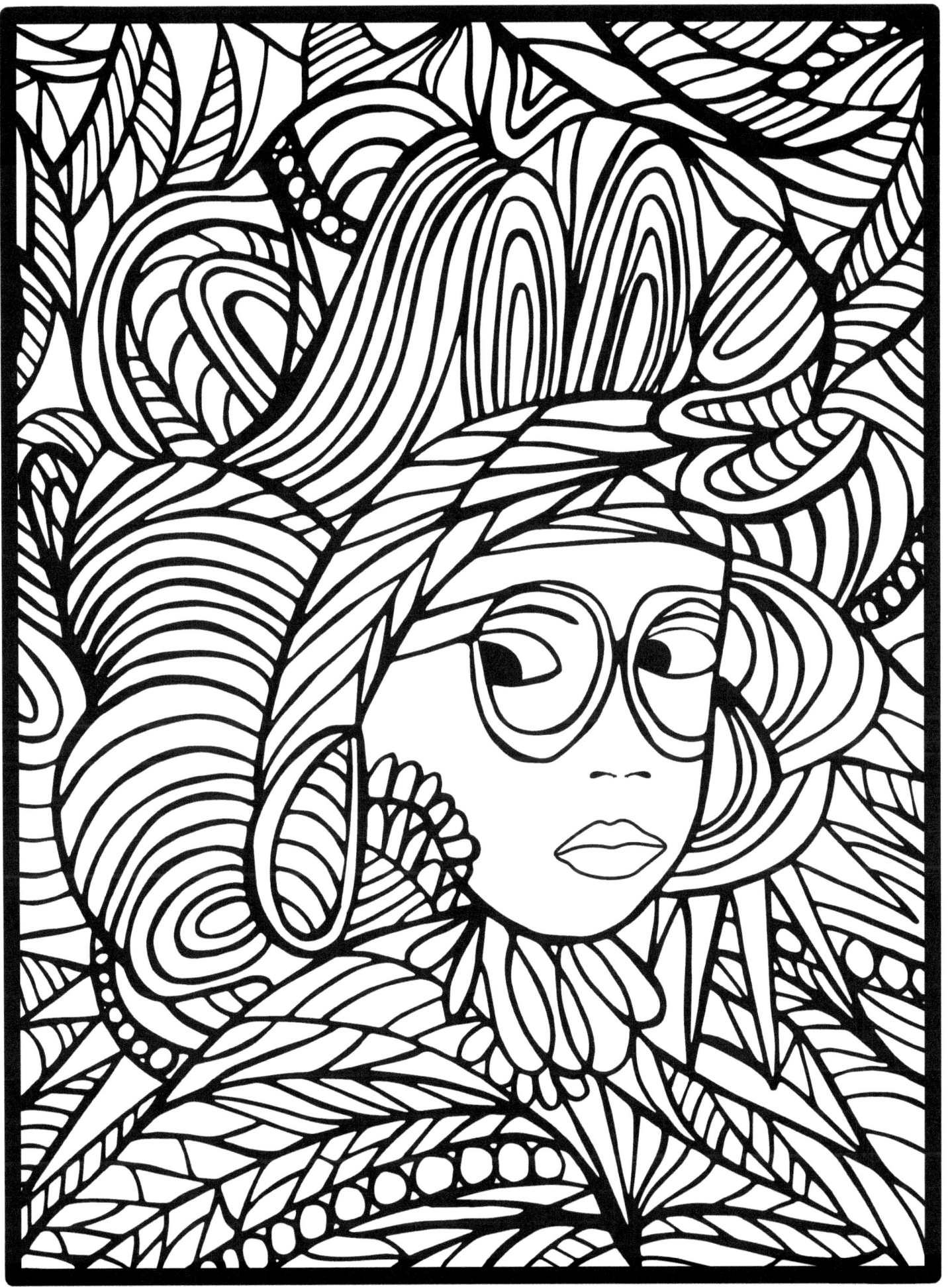

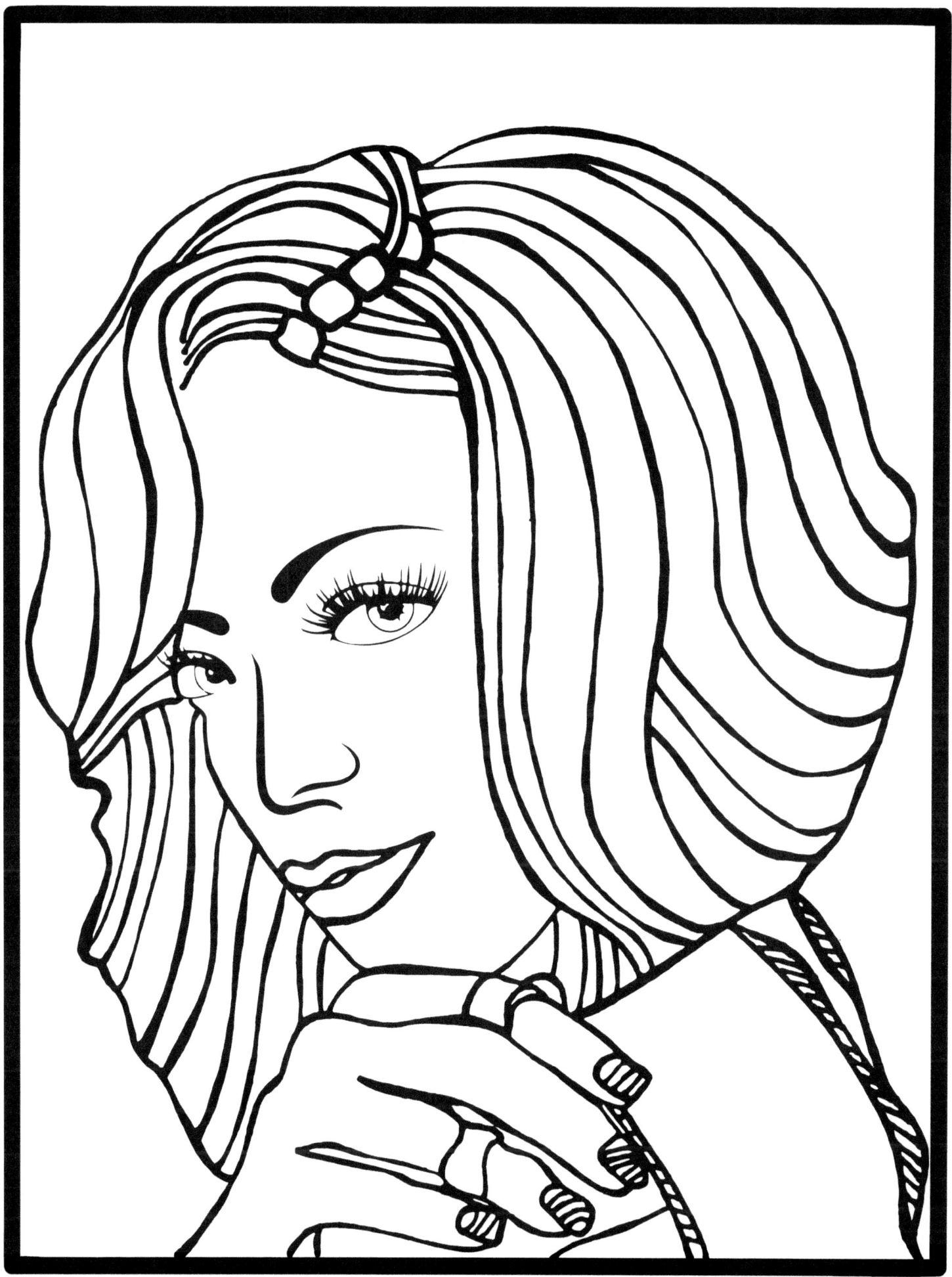

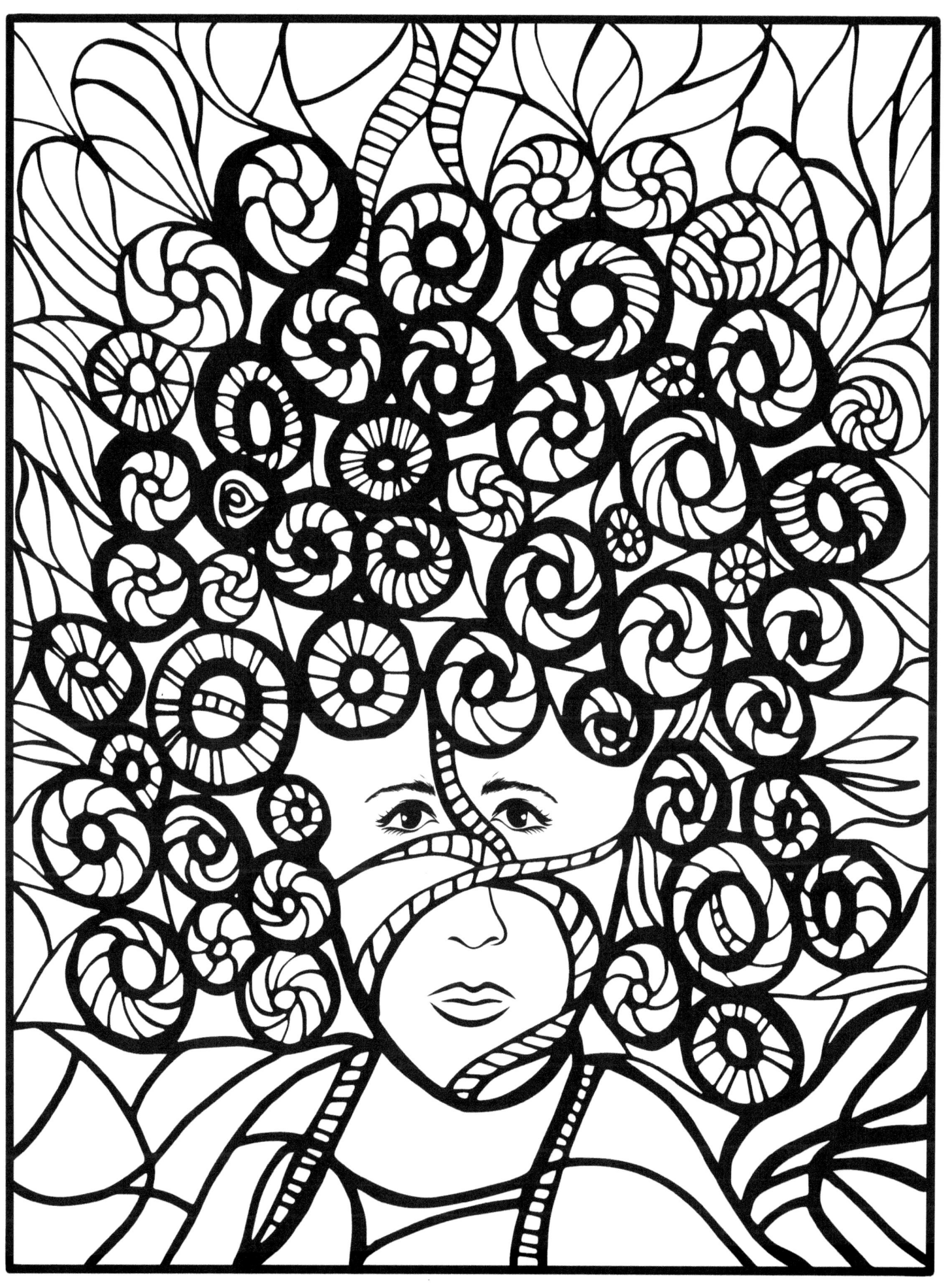

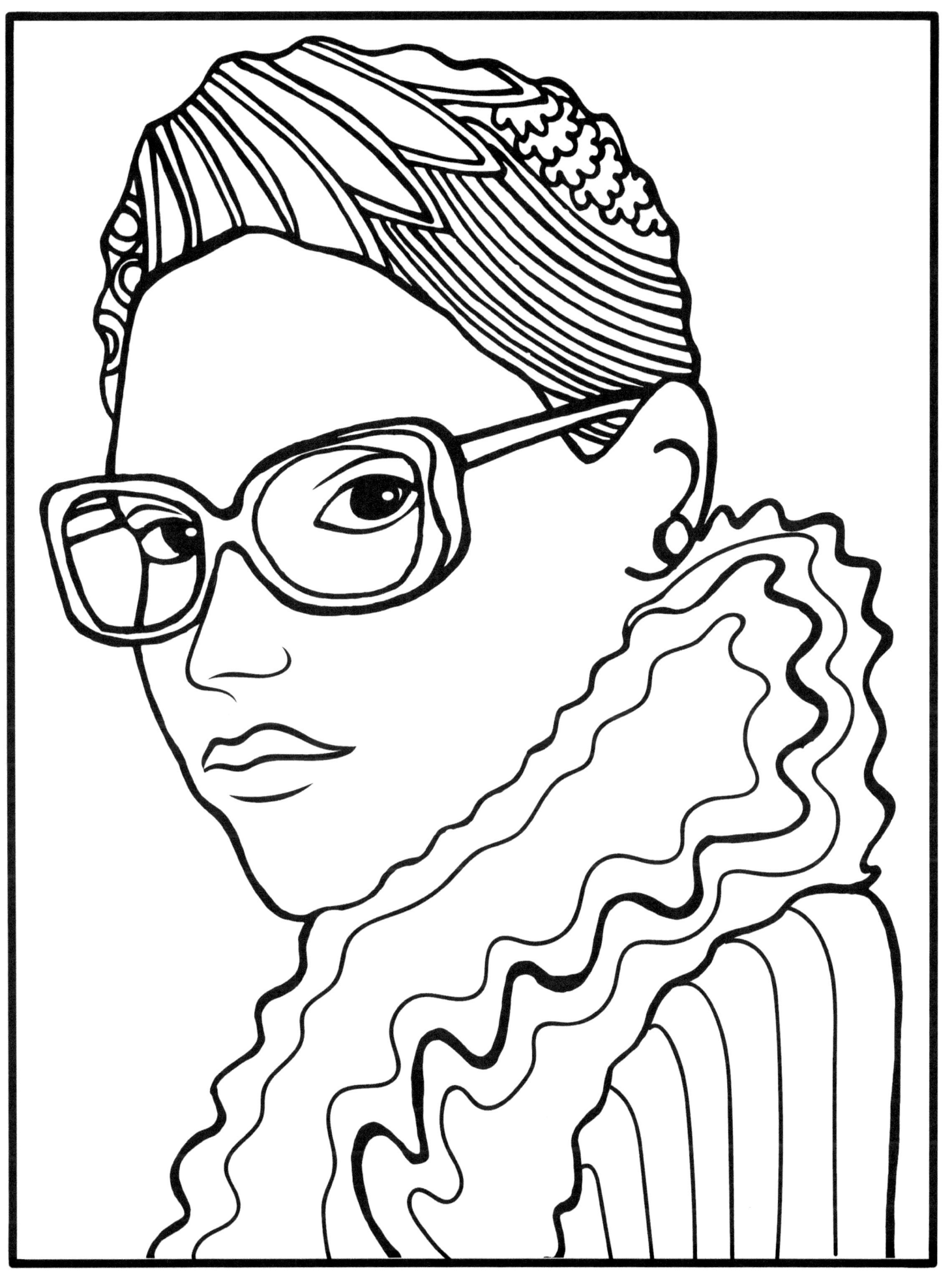

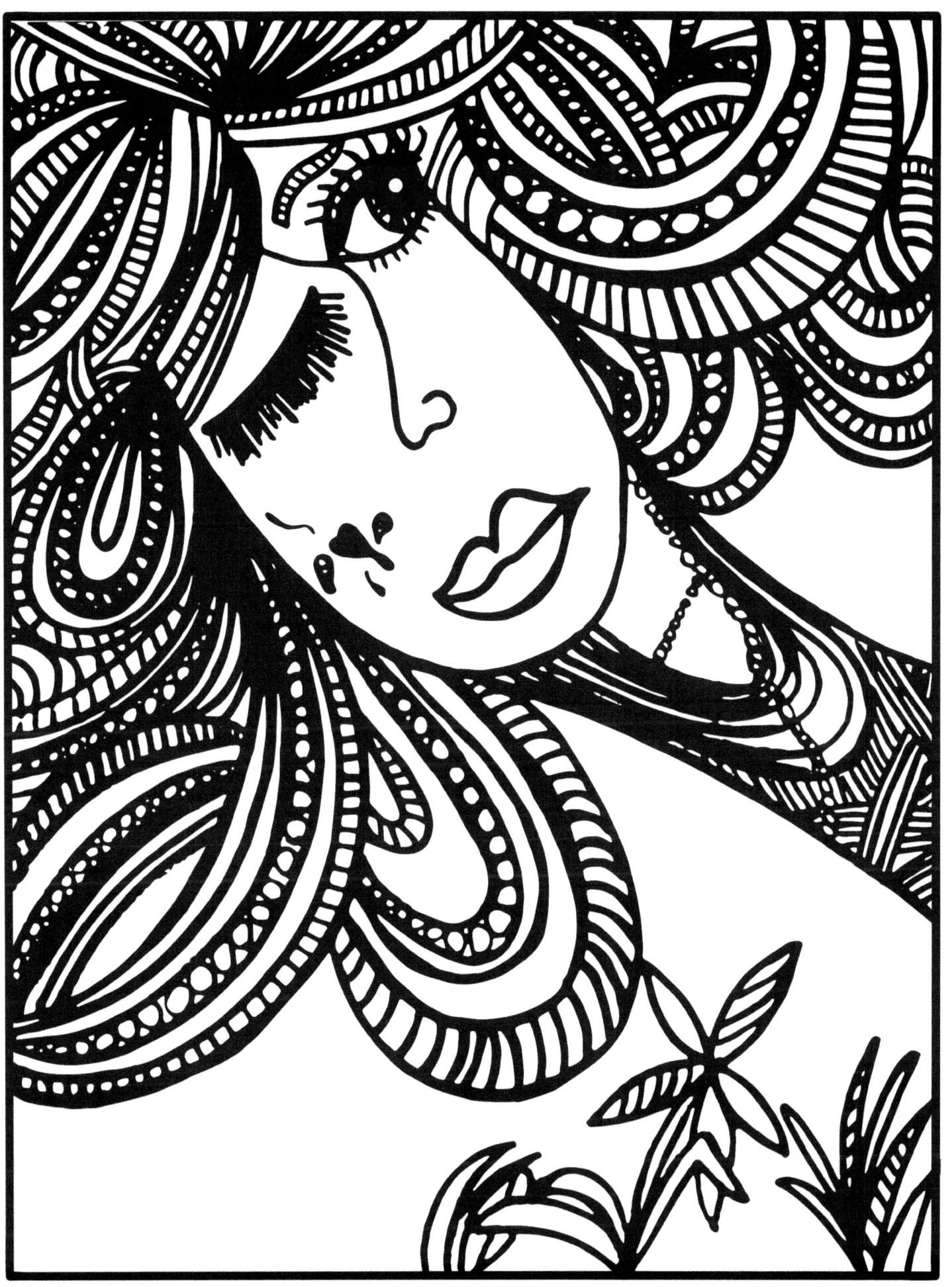

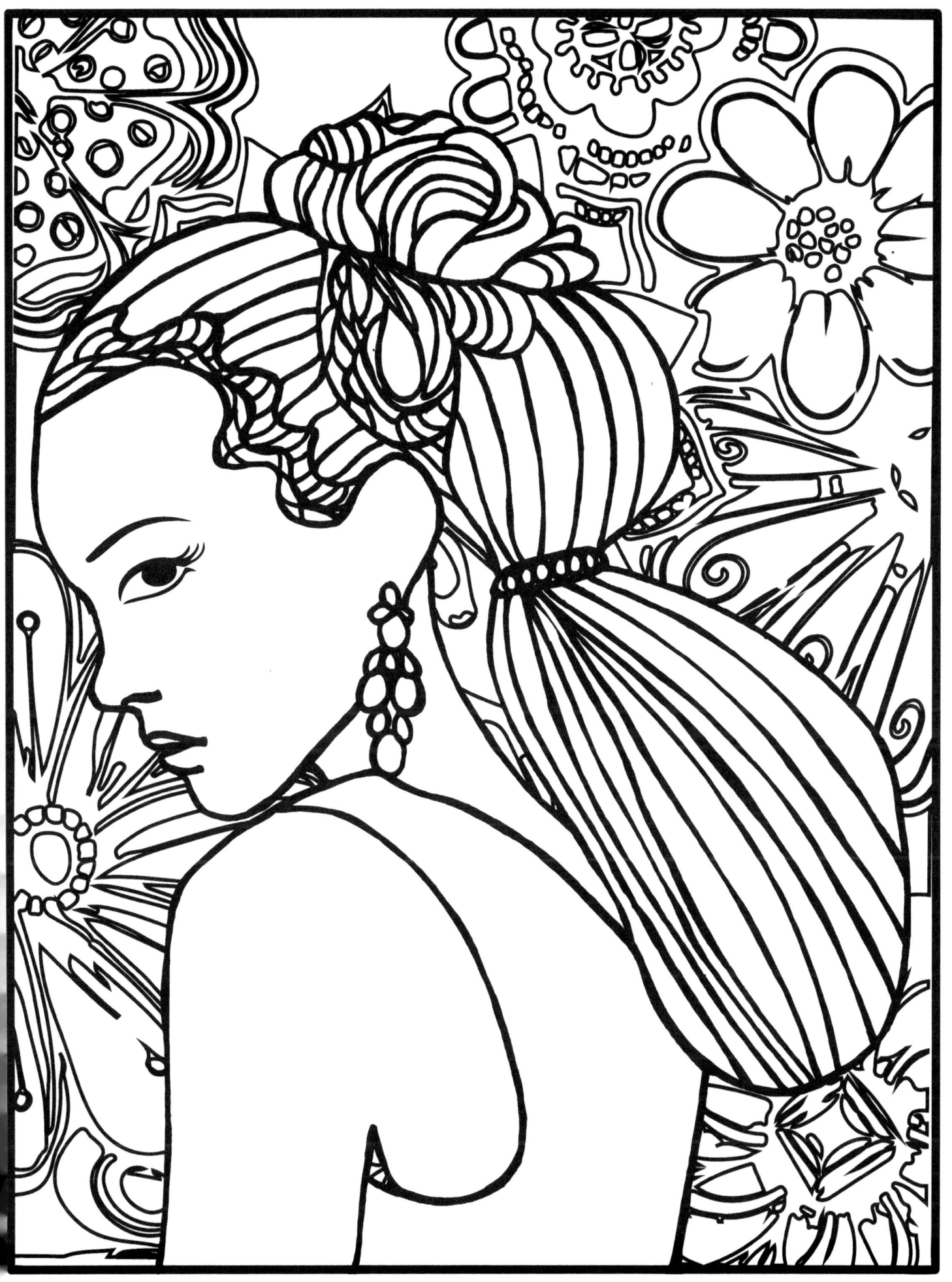

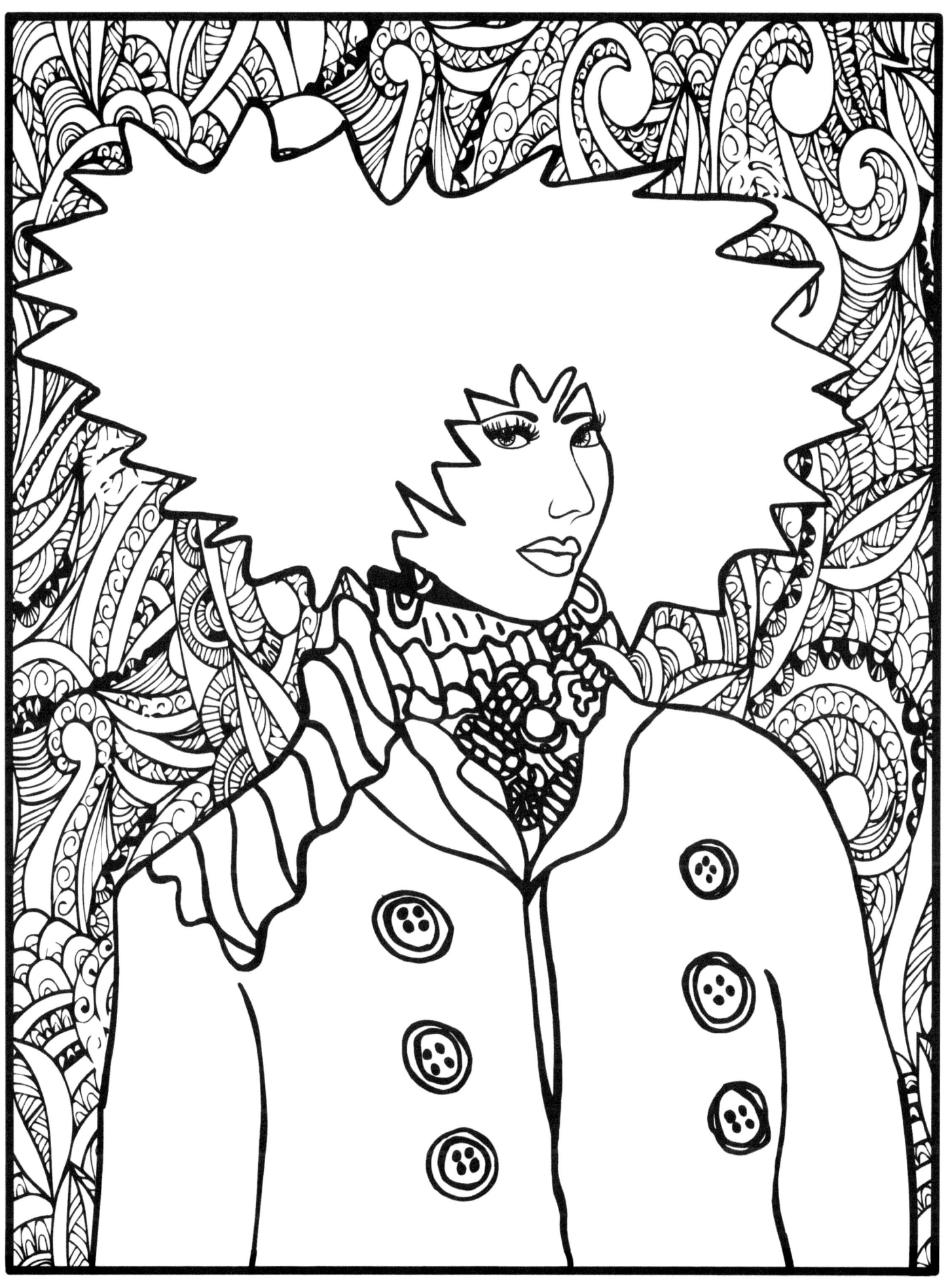

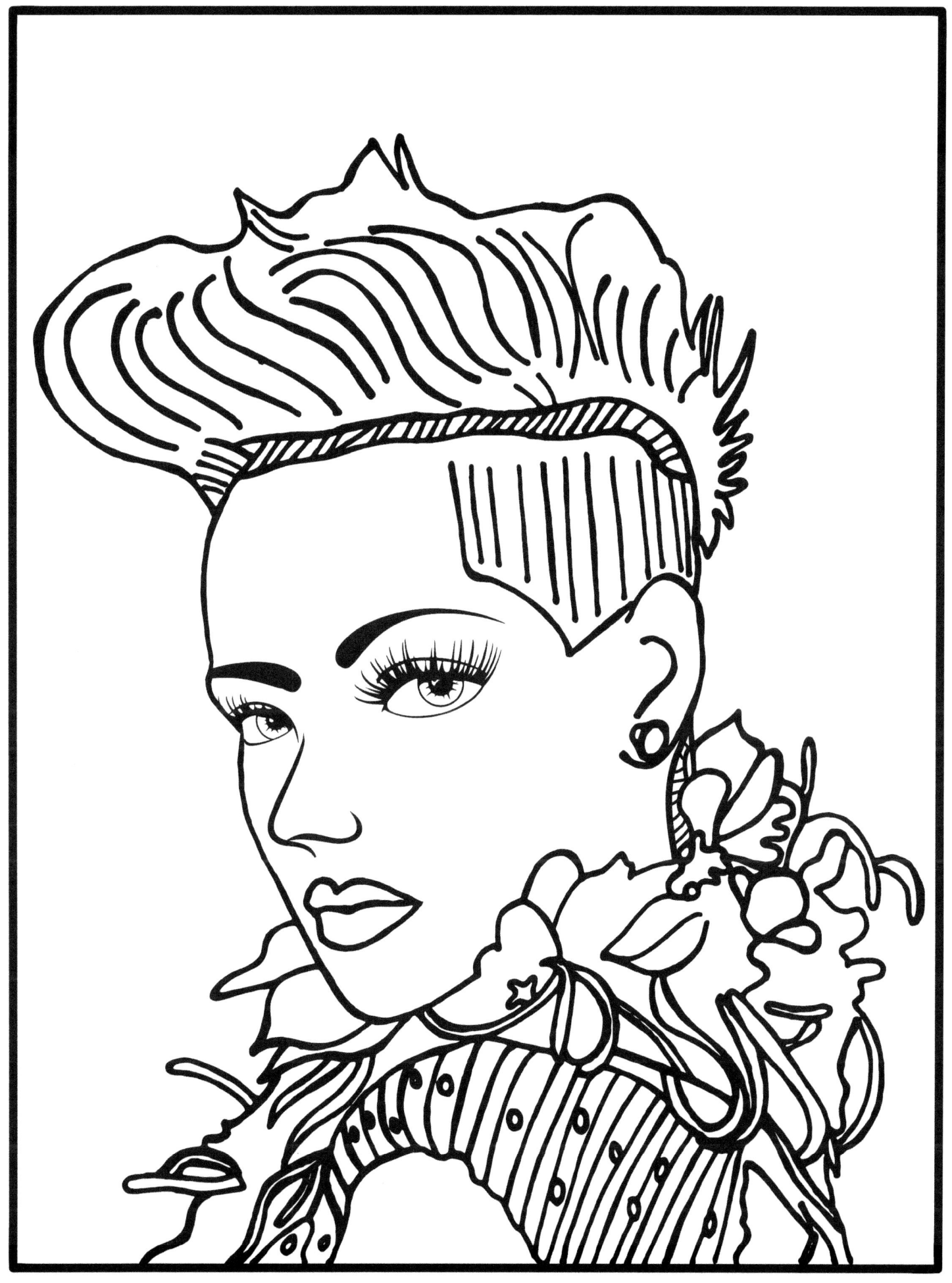

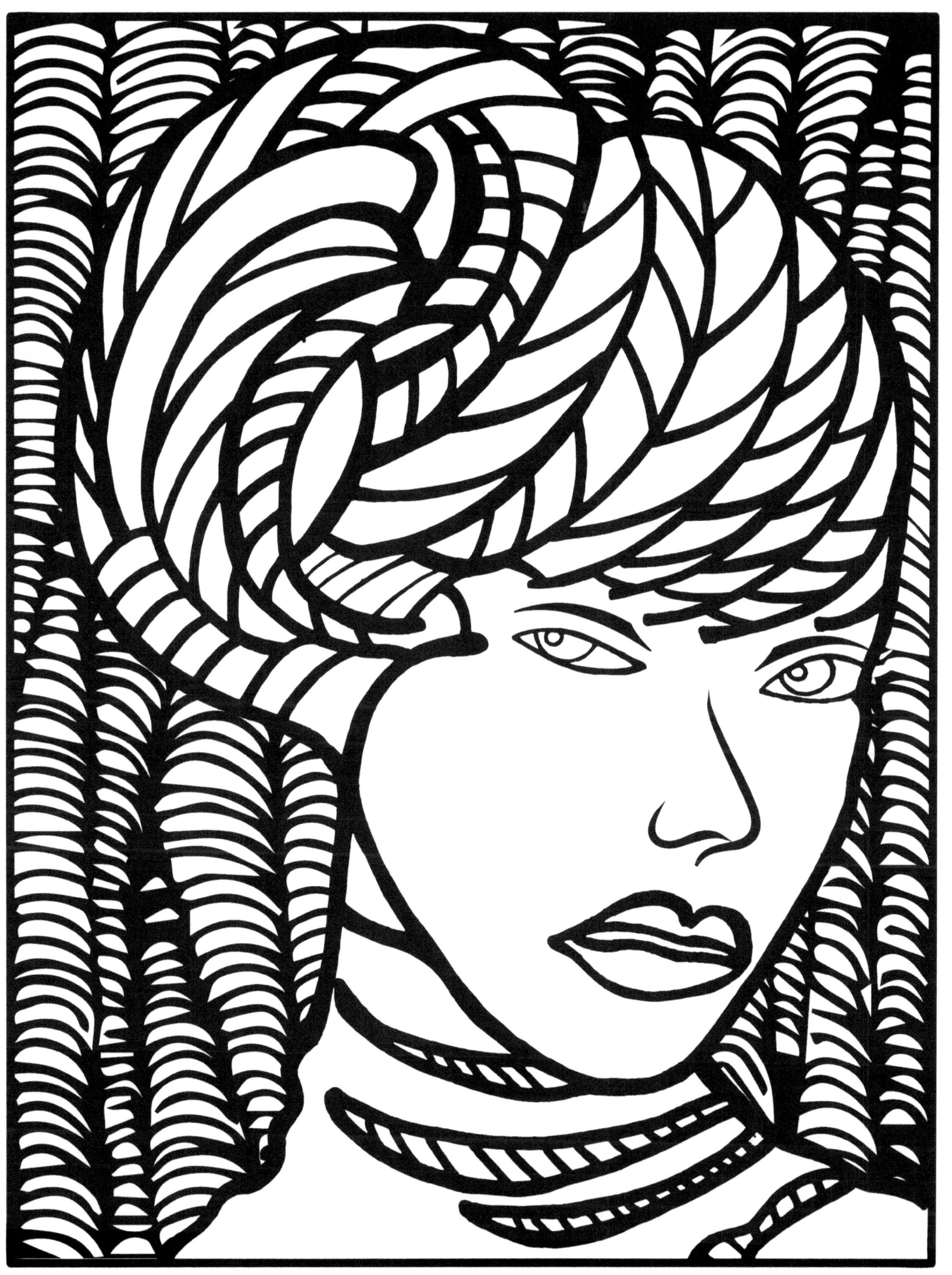

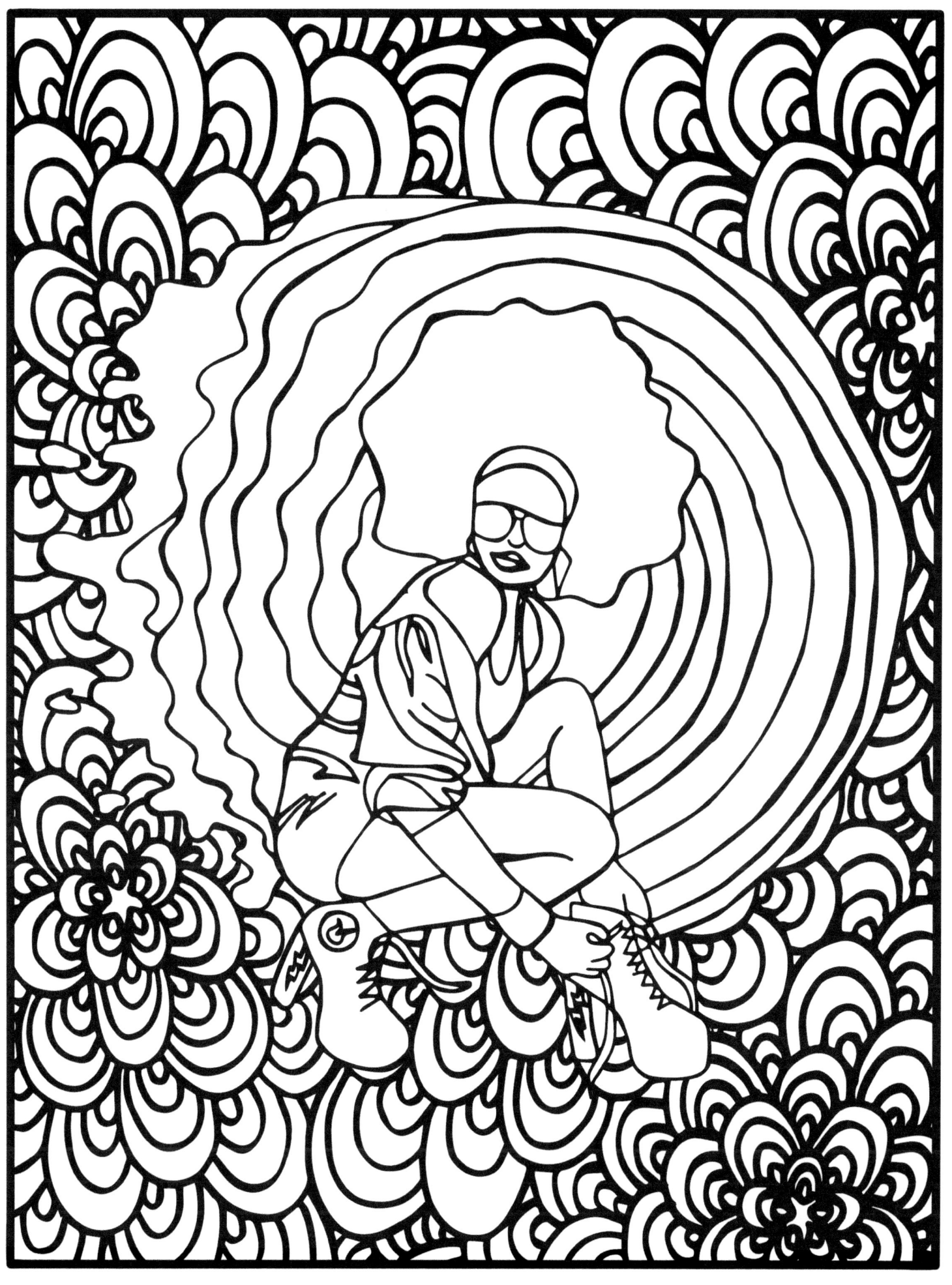

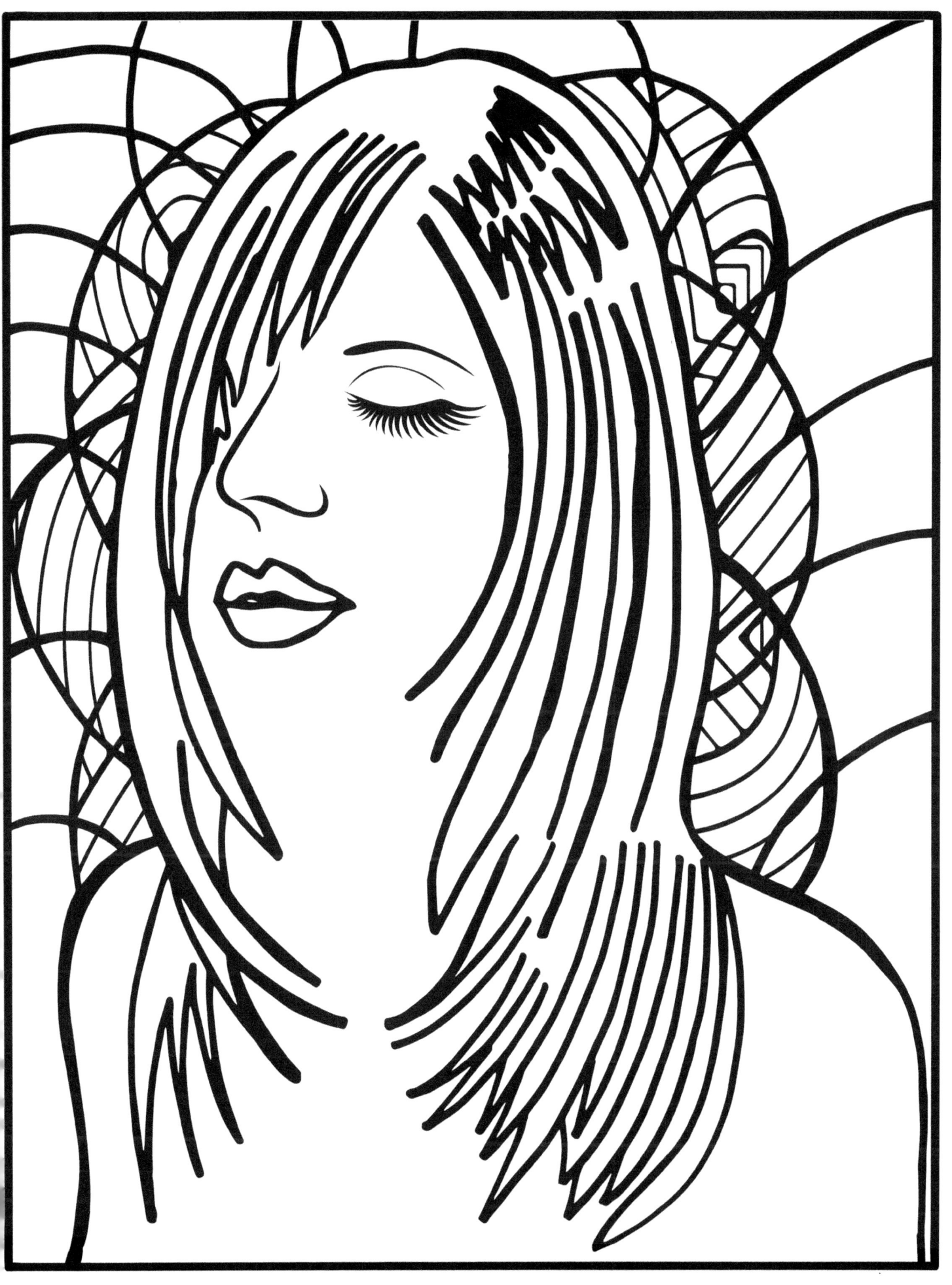

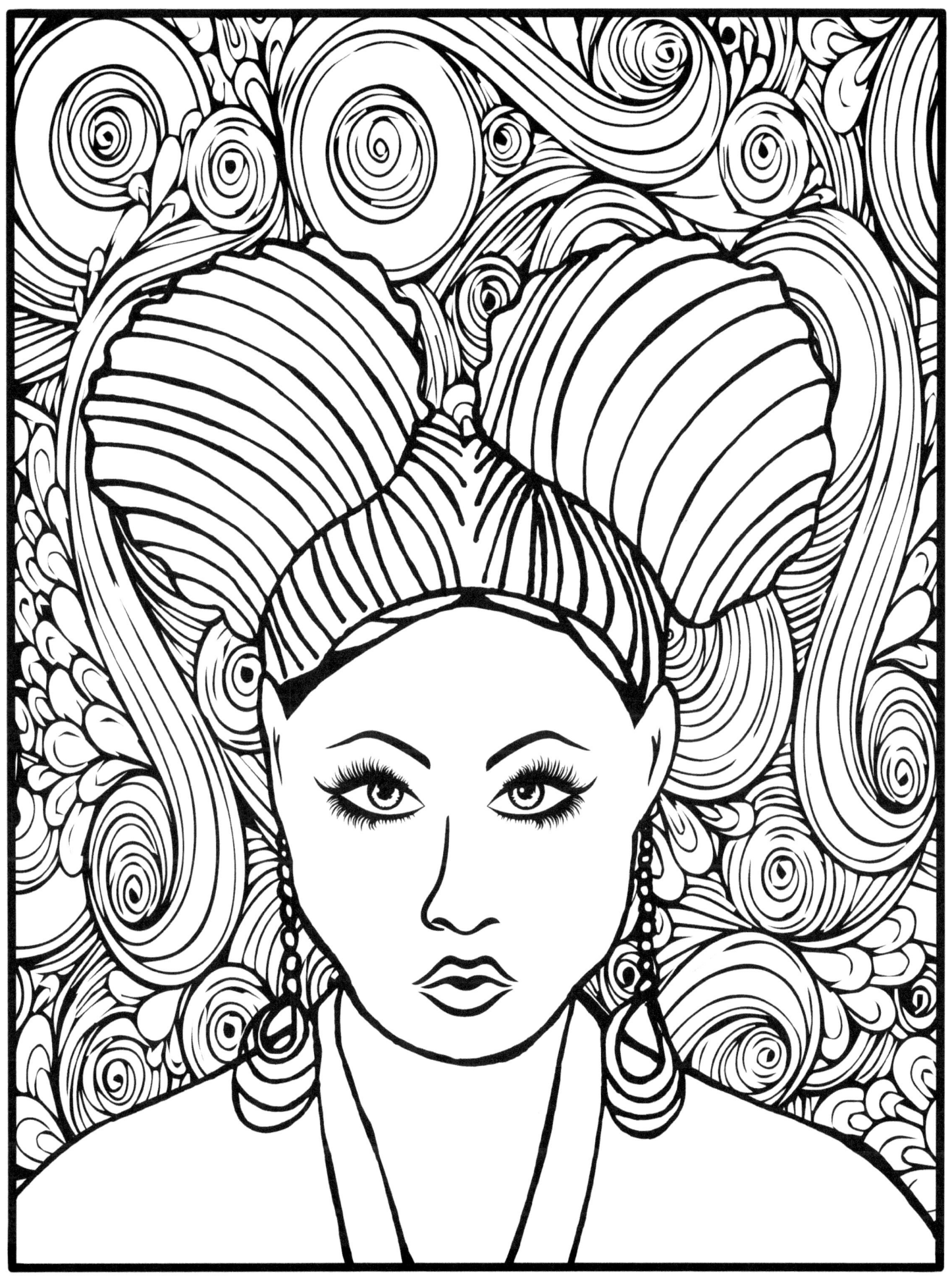

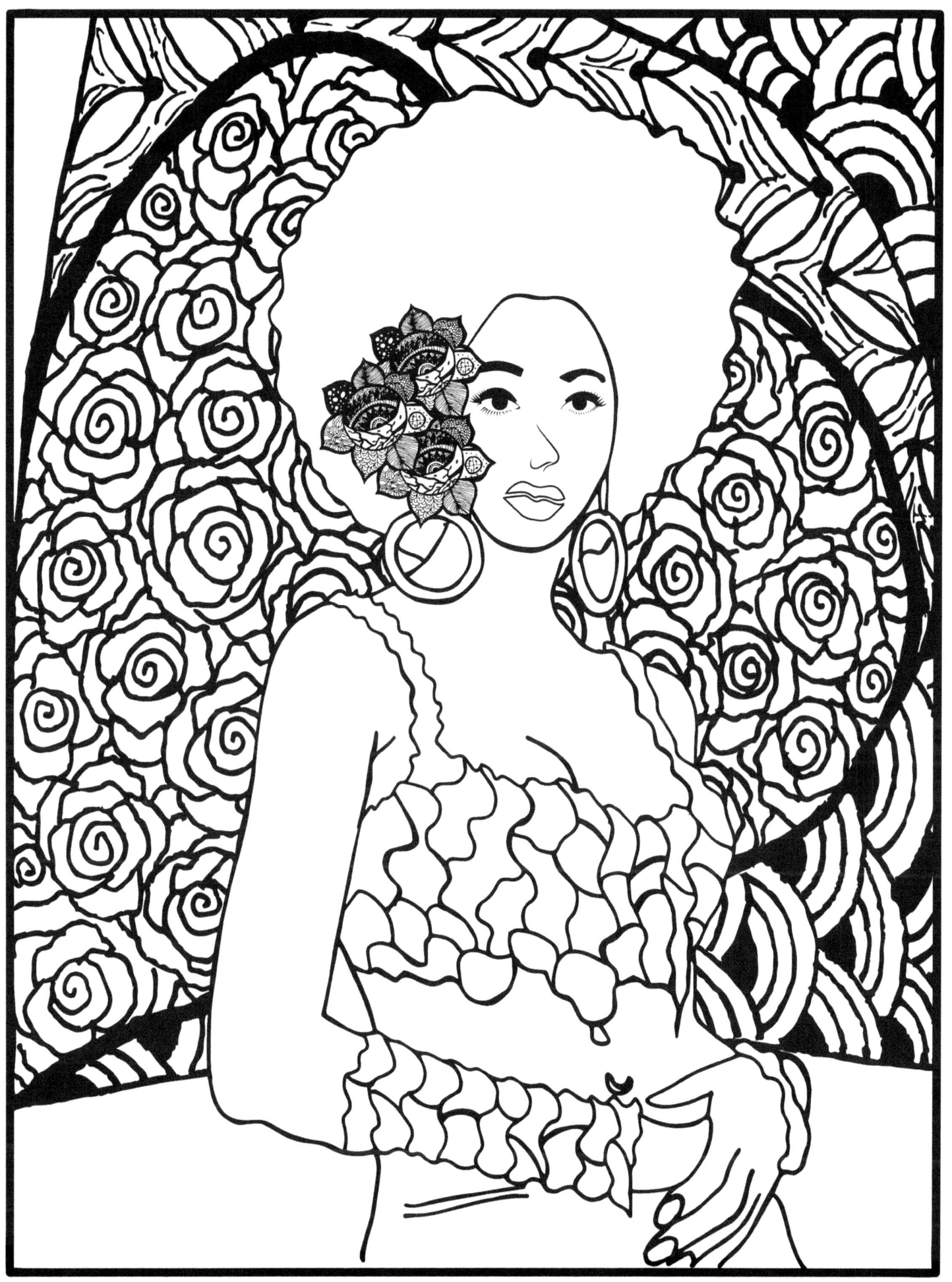

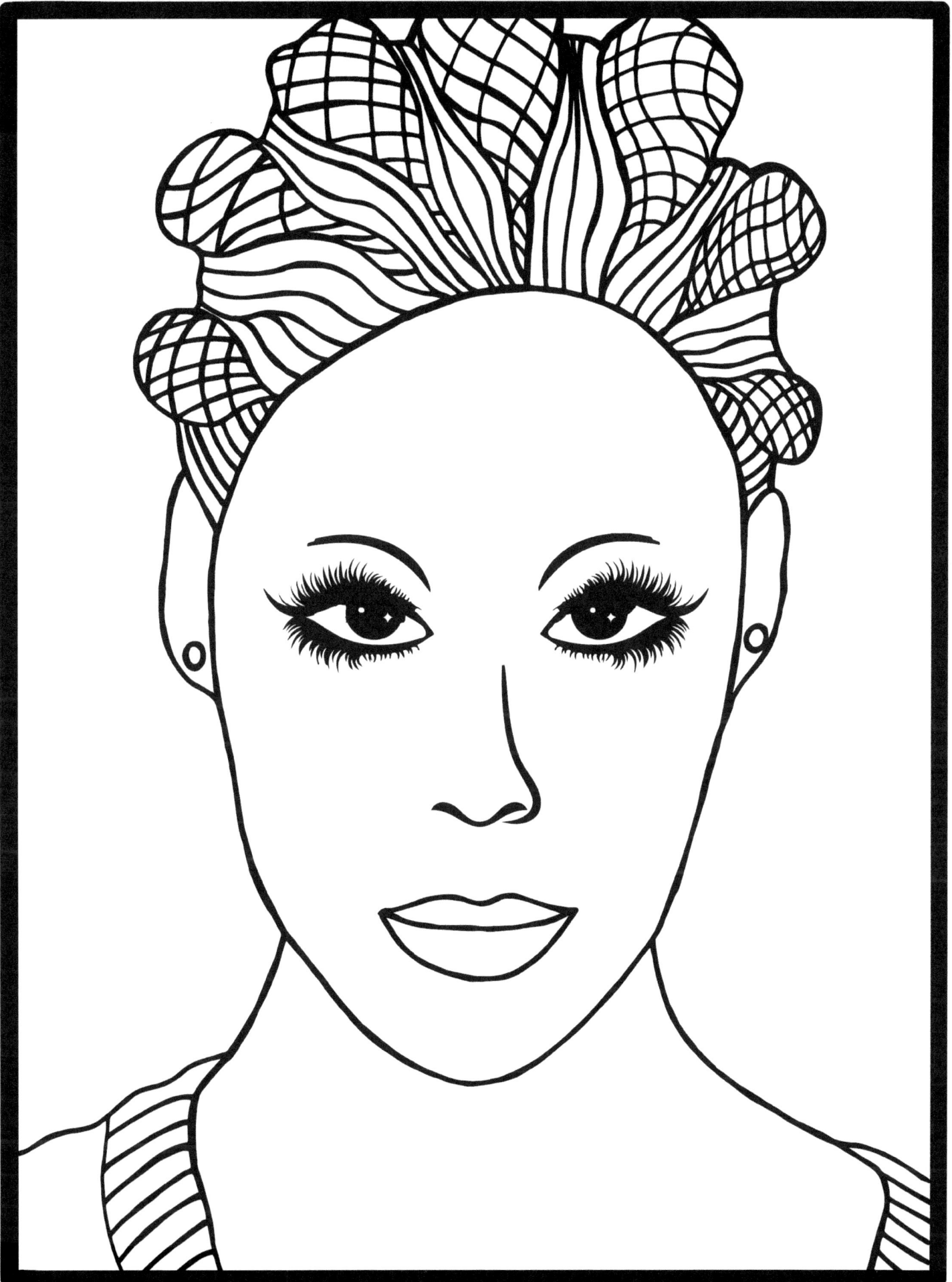

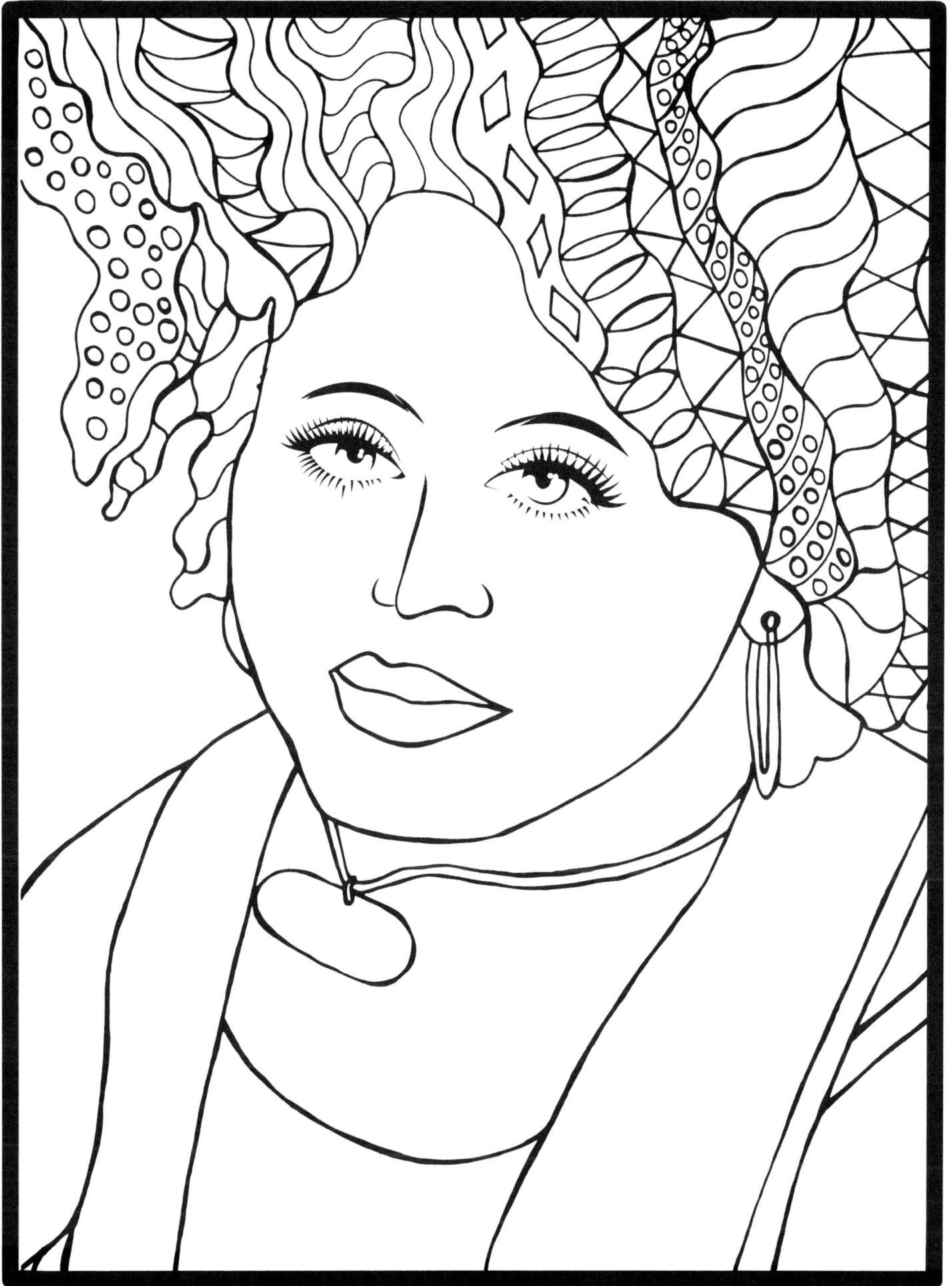

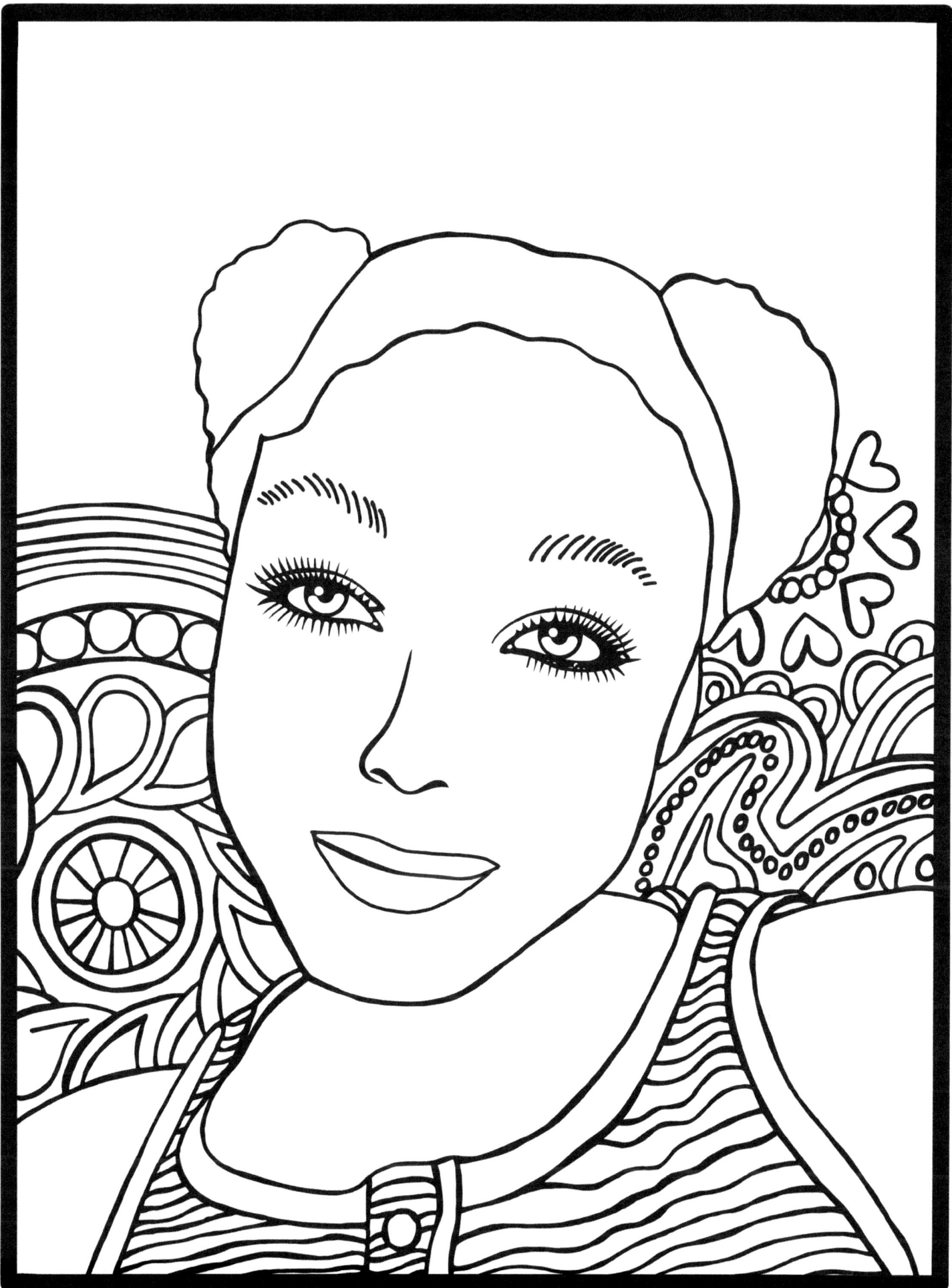

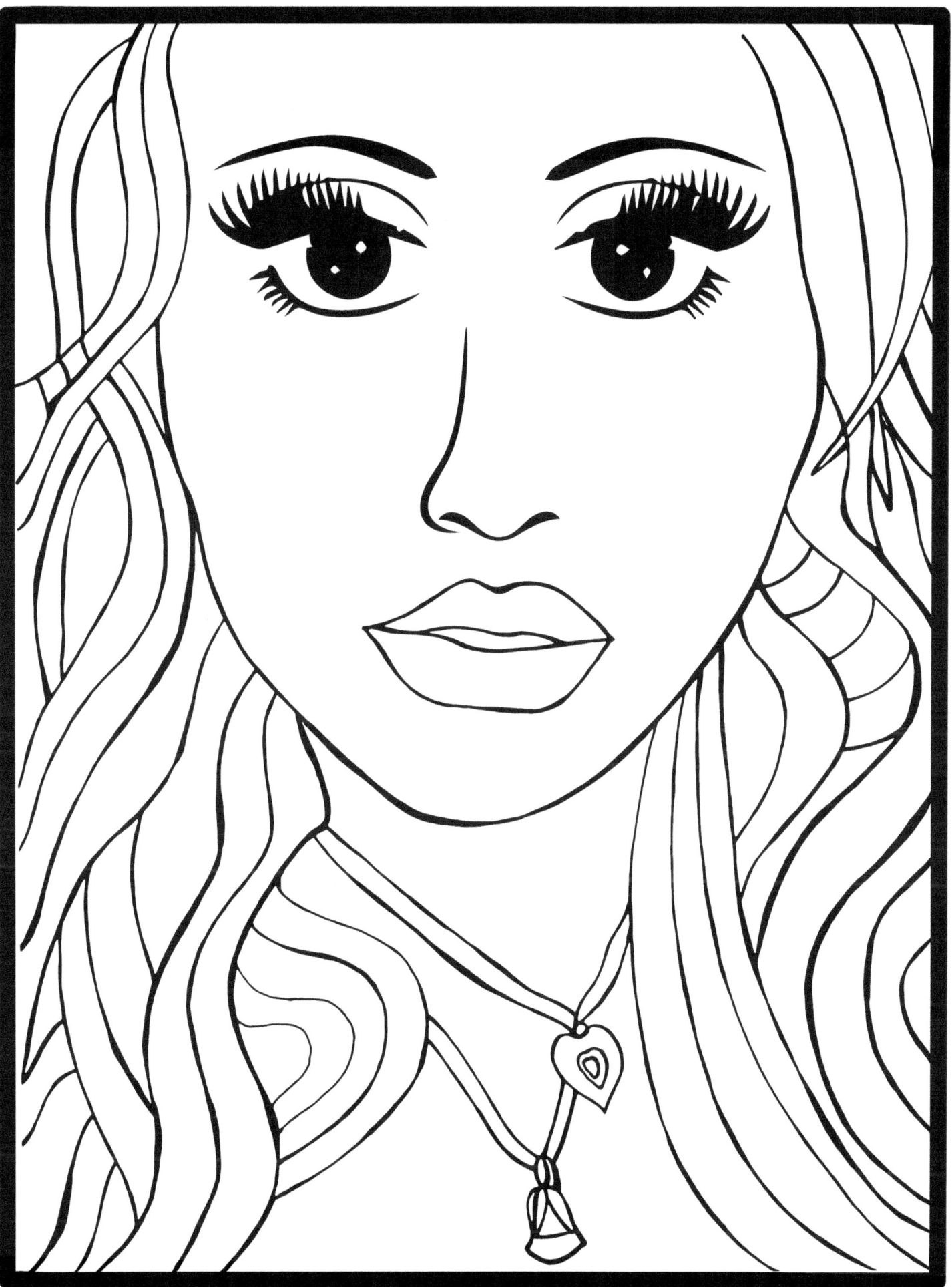

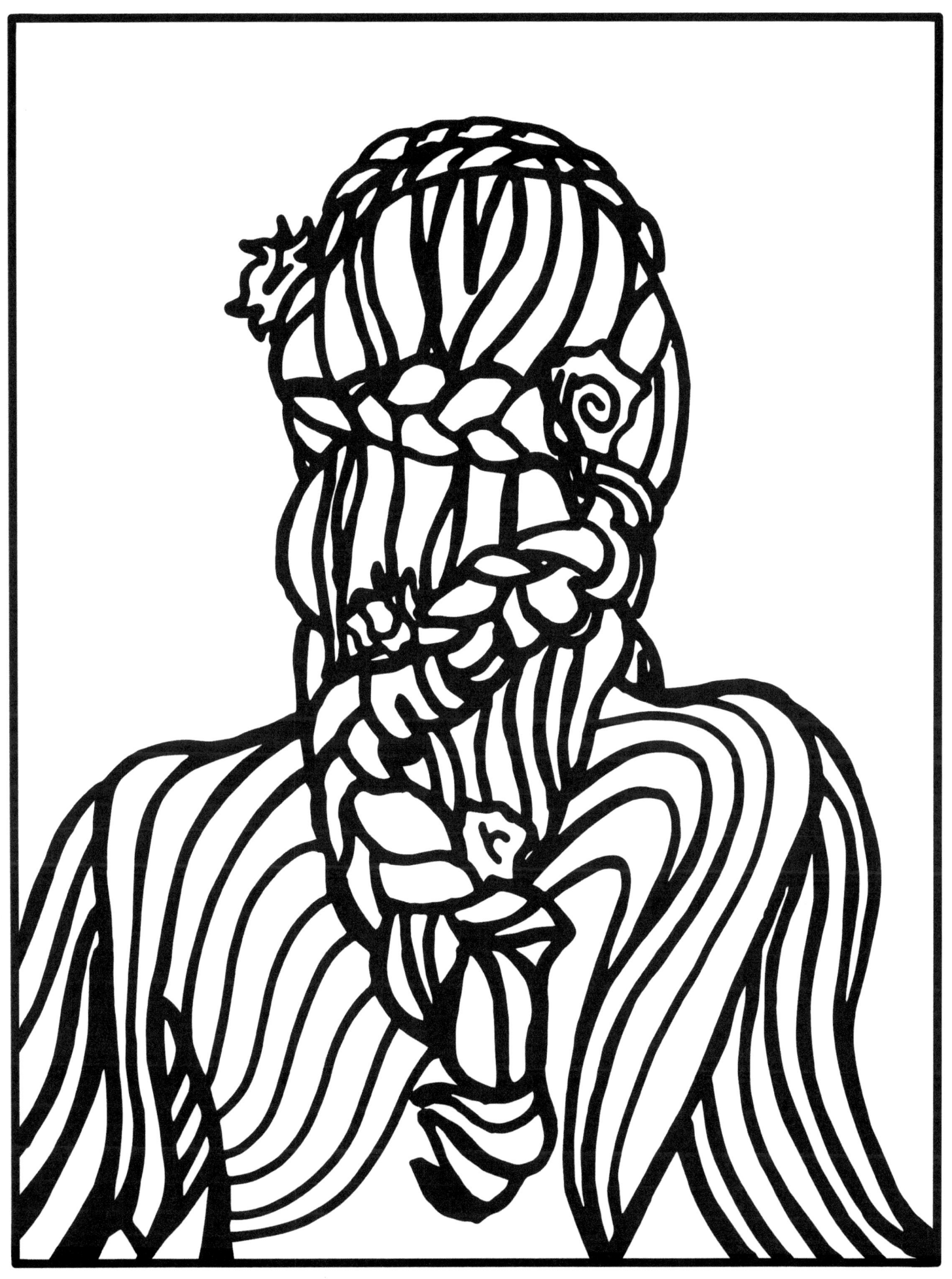

DOODLE DIVA

line drawings allow you to unleash your inner Child and travel to a Safe emotionally stress-free

PLACE

www.ingramcontent.com/pod-product-compliance
Lightning Source LLC
Chambersburg PA
CBHW080603190526
45169CB00007B/2865